To Joa ♡ **YO-ARC-997**
at "Whatever age" - think
of the words of George
Burns - p. 87

Love,
Louise Weaver

Joanna,
     Page 37 -
Happy Birthday
and thanks for
always listening.
          Love,
          Barb

DELANEY
STREET
PRESS

Have a Happy Birthday... You Deserve It!

Have a Happy Birthday...
You Deserve It!

*Compiled and Edited
by Criswell Freeman*

©2000 by Walnut Grove Press

All rights reserved. Except for brief quotes used in reviews, articles, or other media, no part of this book may be reproduced or transmitted in any form or by any means, electronic or mechanical, including photocopying, recording, or by information storage or retrieval system, without permission by the publisher.

DELANEY STREET PRESS
Nashville, TN 37205
800-256-8584

ISBN 1-58334-061-1

The ideas expressed in this book are not, in all cases, exact quotations, as some have been edited for clarity and brevity. In all cases, the author has attempted to maintain the speaker's original intent. In some cases, material for this book was obtained from secondary sources, primarily print media. While every effort was made to ensure the accuracy of these sources, the accuracy cannot be guaranteed. For additions, deletions, corrections or clarifications in future editions of this text, please write DELANEY STREET PRESS.

Printed in the United States of America
Cover Design by Bart Dawson
Typesetting & Page Layout by Criswell Freeman

1 2 3 4 5 6 7 8 9 10 • 00 01 02 03 04 05 06

ACKNOWLEDGMENTS

The author gratefully acknowledges the helpful support of Angela Beasley Freeman, Dick and Mary Freeman, Carlisle and Claudette Beasley, Jim Gallery, Mary Susan Freeman, and the entire team of helpful professionals at both Walnut Grove Press and Delaney Street Press.

For Claudette Beasley

Table of Contents

A Birthday Message to Readers

If you're celebrating another year of life, congratulations! No doubt you've earned the right to enjoy a wonderful party, and this little book is intended to add to that enjoyment.

On the following pages, you'll encounter a collection of profound ideas from some of history's greatest thinkers. These quotations are intended to make you smile and make you think.

Robert Louis Stevenson wisely observed, "There is no duty so much underrated as the duty of being happy." So on this special occasion, do your duty and have a very happy birthday. You deserve it!

1

Have a Happy Birthday...
You Deserve It!

Michel de Montaigne noted, "The clearest sign of wisdom is continued cheerfulness." These words have a special meaning on this special day: your birthday. So why not celebrate wisely by practicing the happiness habit?

Your happiness depends upon how you think and what you do. So do yourself a favor by thinking good thoughts and doing good deeds. If you do, every day will be a cause for celebration.

Happiness
is a habit.
Cultivate it.

Elbert Hubbard

One cannot have too large a party.

Jane Austen

Life is a journey,
   not a destination; and happiness
      is not "there" but here;
      not tomorrow, but today.

Sidney Greenberg

Most people are about as happy
   as they make up their minds to be.

Abraham Lincoln

Brief is the space of life
   allotted to you; pass it as pleasantly
      as you can, not grieving
         from noon till eve.

Euripides

P eople miss their share of happiness,
not because they never found it, but
because they didn't stop to enjoy it.

William Feather

H appiness is a matter of
your own doing. You can be happy
or you can be unhappy. It's
just according to the way you
look at things.

Walt Disney

T hink contentment
the greatest wealth.

George Shelley

Finish every day and be done
with it. You have done what you
could; some blunders and
absurdities have crept in; forget
them as soon as you can.

Ralph Waldo Emerson

The growth of wisdom
may be gauged accurately by
the decline of ill-temper.

Nietzsche

Anger tortures itself.

Publilius Syrus

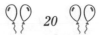

The longer we
dwell on our
misfortunes,
the greater is
their power
to harm us.

Voltaire

Happiness is not a state to arrive at, but a manner of traveling.

Samuel Johnson

Nothing is good or bad but
thinking makes it so.
William Shakespeare

Do not let trifles disturb
your tranquillity. Life is too
precious to be sacrificed
for the nonessential and
the transient. Ignore
the inconsequential.
Grenville Kleiser

Contentment is a
perishable commodity. That's
what makes it so precious.
Burgess Meredith

Happiness means having
  something to do and
  something to live for.

Bishop Fulton J. Sheen

Is not life a hundred times
too short for us to bore ourselves?

Nietzsche

Whatever you do, do it
  with all your heart and soul.

Bernard Baruch

An inexhaustible good nature is one of the most precious gifts of heaven.

Washington Irving

2

Have Fun

On your birthday, you deserve to have fun and lots of it! It's a day to celebrate the successful completion of yet another year.

Enjoying your birthday (along with the other 364 days of the year) is an obligation that you owe to yourself. So take time today for a heaping helping of good, clean, soul-stirring fun. You've earned it.

A sad soul can
  kill you quicker than a germ.
                    John Steinbeck

B e. Live. And don't worry
    too much about the troubles
      that loom so large today.
        They will pass.
                    Mickey Rooney

D o not borrow trouble by
    dreading tomorrow. It is the
  dark menace of the future that
      makes cowards of us all.
                    Dorothy Dix

Laugh and the
world laughs
with you.
Weep and you
weep alone.

Ella Wheeler Wilcox

Life is 10 percent what you make it and 90 percent how you take it.

Irving Berlin

Happiness depends,
as Nature shows,
Less on exterior things
than most suppose.

William Cowper

To love what you do
and feel that it matters —
how could anything else
be more fun?

Katharine Graham

This is the true joy in life:
being used for a purpose
recognized by yourself
as a mighty one.

George Bernard Shaw

Life consists less in length
of days than in the keen
sense of living.

Jean-Jacques Rousseau

Wrinkles should
merely indicate
where smiles
have been.

Mark Twain

3

It's Your Party: Invite Your Friends

Robert Louis Stevenson wrote, "A friend is a present you give yourself." Those words are especially true on a birthday, most notably yours.

Birthdays are meant to be shared with friends, so why not invite the whole gang over to celebrate your big day? Then, with all your pals in attendance, you can remind yourself of a wonderful gift that you've already given yourself: your friends.

There is nothing on this
earth more to be prized than
true friendship.

St. Thomas Aquinas

A friend is one who
makes me do my best.

Oswald Chambers

A sympathetic friend can be
quite as dear as a brother.

Homer

Man's best support is a very dear friend.

Cicero

The language of
friendship is
not words,
but meanings.

Henry David Thoreau

...You Deserve It!

W e have no more right
to consume happiness without
producing it than to consume
wealth without producing it.

George Bernard Shaw

A true friend is the most
precious of all possessions and
the one we often take the least
thought about acquiring.

La Rochefoucauld

W here there are friends,
there is wealth.

Latin Proverb

Shared joys make a friend,
   not shared sufferings.

Goethe

The only way to have a friend
   is to be one.

Ralph Waldo Emerson

The comfort of having a friend
may be taken away, but not that
   of having had one.

Seneca

What is a friend? A single soul dwelling in two bodies.

Aristotle

It is more shameful to distrust
our friends than to be deceived
by them.

La Rochefoucauld

The ornaments of our house
are the friends who frequent it.

Ralph Waldo Emerson

Friendships form among people
who strengthen one another.

Franklin Owen

Cheerful company shortens the miles.

German Proverb

4

Another Year Wiser

As the calendar ticks off one more year, it's time to reflect on lessons learned. How have you spent the last year? What have you learned and how have you used your new-found knowledge? In what ways have you improved yourself, and what are your plans to continue your personal growth? Are you blossoming with age? Hopefully so.

This birthday, take a solemn pledge to keep learning and to keep growing. Because, as fast-food pioneer Ray Kroc correctly observed, "If you're green you're growing, if you're ripe you rot!"

Man's main task in life is giving birth to himself.

Erich Fromm

The art of living lies
less in eliminating our troubles
than in growing with them.

Bernard Baruch

All growth is a leap in the dark.

Henry Miller

Be not afraid of growing slowly,
be afraid only of
standing still.

Chinese Proverb

The education of a man
is completed only
when he dies.

Robert E. Lee

I grow old ever learning
many things.

Solon

You don't grow old.
When you cease to grow,
you *are* old.

Charles Judson Herrick

If you do what you've
always done, you'll get
what you always got.

Anonymous

Nothing endures but change.

Heraclitus

Only in growth, reform,
and change, paradoxically
enough, is true security found.

Anne Morrow Lindbergh

Have a Happy Birthday...

The days in my life that stand out
most vividly are the days
I've learned something.
Learning is so exciting
I get goose bumps.

Lucille Ball

Growth is the only evidence of life.
John Henry Cardinal Newman

Happiness to me means
constant growth.

Eddie Albert

Adapt or perish,
now as ever,
is nature's
inexorable
imperative.

H. G. Wells

Have a Happy Birthday...

It is better to wear out
than to rust.

Richard Cumberland

Anyone who stops learning
is old, whether at twenty
or eighty.

Henry Ford

I am long on ideas but short
on time. I expect to live to be
only about a hundred.

Thomas Edison

We are constantly becoming what eventually we are going to be.

Samuel Johnson

As long as you live,
    keep learning *how* to live.

Seneca

I am still learning.

Michelangelo's Motto

A man, though wise,
    should never be ashamed
        of learning more.

Sophocles

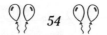

In youth we learn. In age we understand.

Marie Ebner-Eschenbach

5

Celebrate Life

Every birthday serves as a gentle reminder that time indeed marches on. Since we can't stop Father Time — or even slow him down for that matter — only one truly intelligent course of action remains: live to the fullest.

If you're treating each new day as a priceless gift, congratulations. If you're taking life for granted, think again.

Today, and tomorrow, and every day after that should be cause for celebration. This day is yours, and what a priceless gift it is.

Live your life and forget your age.

Frank Bering

Find the journey's end in every step.

Ralph Waldo Emerson

Life is short. Make the most
of the present.

Marcus Aurelius

Life is in the living, in the tissue
of every day and hour.

Stephen Leacock

Do not act as if you had a thousand years to live.

Marcus Aurelius

Do something worth remembering.

Elvis Presley

Dying seems less sad than
    having lived too little.

Gloria Steinem

The great use of life is to spend it
    for something that will outlast it.

William James

The real fear is not death — it is
    the fear of wasting life.

Jackie Gleason

The Bird of Time has
but a little way to flutter —
and the bird is on the wing.

Omar Khayyám

Life has got to be lived.
That's all there is to it.

Eleanor Roosevelt

Life is what we make it.
Always has been.
Always will be.

Grandma Moses

May you live
all the days
of your life.

Jonathan Swift

Time is really the only capital that any human being has and the only thing he can't afford to lose.

Thomas Edison

Tomorrow's life is too late. Live today.

Martial

The passing minute is every man's equal possession.

Marcus Aurelius

Time is so precious that God deals it out only second by second.

Bishop Fulton J. Sheen

Don't believe there's plenty of time for everything. There isn't.

Lillian Hellman

What we are
is God's gift to us.
What we become
is our gift to God.

Eleanor Powell

6

Young at Heart

Okay, the calendar says you're another year older. And you know it must be true, because people are singing *Happy Birthday to You* while bringing out a cake with enough candles to light a small office building. But the real issue on this day is not your age, it's your attitude.

By maintaining a youthful outlook, you'll be giving yourself the birthday gift that keeps on giving. So ignore the number of candles on the cake, and think only of the flame that burns brightly in your heart; *that's* the fire that should never go out.

Every child is an artist.
   The problem is how to remain
   an artist once he grows up.

Pablo Picasso

Middle age is when you don't have
   to have fun to enjoy yourself.

Franklin P. Jones

Cherish all your happy moments.
They make a fine cushion for old age.

Christopher Morley

Genius is childhood recaptured.

Charles Baudelaire

It is not how many years we live, but what we do with them.

Evangeline Booth

Life is available
to anyone no matter
what age. All you have
to do is grab it.

Art Carney

Life is no brief candle to me.
It is a sort of splendid torch
which I have got hold of for the
moment, and I want to make it
burn as brightly as possible
before handing it on
to future generations.

George Bernard Shaw

Life is either
a daring adventure
or nothing.

Helen Keller

Life, like every
other blessing,
derives its value
from its use alone.

Samuel Johnson

Take a chance. All life is a chance.
Dale Carnegie

Life shrinks or expands
in proportion to one's courage.
Anaïs Nin

Learn what you are and be such.
Pindar

The tragedy of life is not so much
what men suffer,
but what they miss.

Thomas Carlyle

Make your life a mission —
not an intermission.

Arnold Glasgow

As soon as you trust yourself,
you will know how to live.

Goethe

Life is doing things, not making things.

Aristotle

The best way to prepare for life is to begin to live.

Elbert Hubbard

Live from miracle to miracle.

Artur Rubinstein

He who desires, but acts not,
breeds pestilence.

William Blake

Plunge boldly into
the thick of life!

Goethe

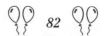

The best way
to make your dreams
come true is
to wake up.

Paul Valéry

One today is worth two tomorrows.

Ben Franklin

This time, like all times,
is a very good one, if we only know
what to do with it.

Ralph Waldo Emerson

Our main business is not to see
what lies dimly at a distance,
but to do what lies
clearly at hand.

Thomas Carlyle

It is *now* and in *this world*
that we must live.

André Gide

All that I know
I learned after thirty.

Georges Clemence

The man of true greatness
never loses his child's heart.

Menc

Youth is the time for adventures
of the body, but age is the time for
triumphs of the mind.

Logan Pearsall Sm

There's an old saying that life begins at 40. That's silly. Life begins every morning when you wake up.

George Burns

Life is painting a picture,
 not doing a sum.

Oliver Wendell Holmes, Jr.

All life is an experiment.
 The more experiments you make,
 the better.

Ralph Waldo Emerson

Do you love life?
 Then do not squander time,
for that's the stuff life is made of.

Ben Franklin

Great minds have purposes, others have wishes.

Washington Irving

The right time is any time
that one is still so lucky
as to have ... Live!

Henry James

No man loves life
like he who is growing old.

Sophocles

Always hold fast to the
present. Every situation, indeed
every moment, is of infinite value,
for it is the representative of a
whole eternity.

Goethe

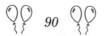

There is no cosmetic like happiness.

Lady Marguerite Blessington

7

Giving Thanks

Birthdays offer many opportunities to say "Thank you." You receive gifts and remembrances from family and friends, and you're appropriately grateful. But a thankful heart was never intended to be locked up in a single day, even a birthday.

This day, like every other, is a wonderful day to stop and count your blessings. Once you start counting, you'll realize that you have been richly blessed. And perhaps, as you make an accounting of your good fortune, you'll feel the urge to cast your eyes upward and say, "Thanks."

God gave you
a gift of
86,400 seconds today.
Have you
used one to say
thank you?

William Arthur Ward

A thankful heart
is not only the
greatest virtue,
but the parent
of all other virtues.

Cicero

Have a Happy Birthday...

No life is so hard that
you can't make it easier
by the way you take it.

Ellen Glasgow

We are all richer
than we think we are.

Michel de Montaigne

Rest and be thankful.

William Wordsworth

Life does not have
to be perfect
to be wonderful.

Annette Funicello

Have a Happy Birthday...

To know how to grow old is
the masterwork of wisdom
and one of the most difficult
chapters in the great art of living.

Henri Frédéric Amiel

The best is yet to be,
The last of life, for which
the first was made.

Robert Browning

At seventy, I would say
the advantage is that you take life
more calmly. You know that
"this too will pass."

Eleanor Roosevelt

A man is not old
until regrets take
the place of dreams.

John Barrymore

Gladly accept the gifts
    of the present hour.

Horace

Count your own blessings and
    let your neighbor count his.

James Thurber

Be content with
    such things as ye have.

Hebrews 13:5

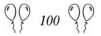 *100*

A grateful mind is a great mind which eventually attracts to itself great things.

Plato

Each day provides its own gifts.

Martial

The greatest gifts are those
we give ourselves.

Sophocles

Gratitude is the most
exquisite form of courtesy.

Jacques Maritain

Joy is the simplest form of
gratitude.

Karl Barth

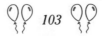 *103*

Write it on your heart that
every day is the best day
of the year.

Ralph Waldo Emerson

Don't complain about getting old.
Many people don't have
that privilege.

Earl Warren

I suppose life is a struggle;
yet, whenever I wake up,
even with a few hours of sleep,
I feel so glad I'm alive.

Jack Benny

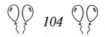

If you love life, life will love you back.

Artur Rubinstein

8

A Great Year Ahead

You've reached another milestone: your birthday. Now it's time to look ahead. No matter how many candles sit atop your cake, there's still much to do. So why not get busy planning your next great adventure?

Each day comes bearing its own special gifts. Your task, of course, is to unwrap those gifts and share them with the world.

The coming year holds great opportunities: Seize them. When you do, you'll make every day a cause for celebration.

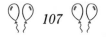

Life is like a
ten-speed bike.
Most of us have
gears we
never use.

Charles Schulz

Whatever you can
do or dream you
can, begin it.
Boldness has
genius, power,
and magic in it.

Goethe

I like dreams of the future better than the history of the past.

Thomas Jefferson

Destiny is not a matter of chance, it is a matter of choice.

William Jennings Bryan

We are all functioning at a small fraction of our capacity. Consequently, the actualizing of our potential can become the most exciting adventure of our lifetime.

Herbert Otto

Life is a series of collisions
with the future; it is not a sum of
what we have been but what we
yearn to be.

José Ortega y Gasset

When a man is willing and
eager, the gods join in.

Aeschylus

Do noble things, do not
dream them all day long.

Charles Kingsley

111

My interest is in the future because I am going to spend the rest of my life there.

Charles F. Kettering

...You Deserve It!

No man need stay the way he is.
Harry Emerson Fosdick

Always be in a state of becoming.
Walt Disney

The best song of your life may be
just around the corner.
Keith Richards

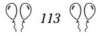 *113*

Don't be afraid to take a big step if one is indicated. You can't cross a chasm in two small jumps.

David Lloyd-George

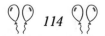

On the human chessboard, all moves are possible.

Miriam Schiff

Have a Happy Birthday...

The mind is like a clock that is constantly running down. It has to be wound up daily with good thoughts.

Bishop Fulton J. Sheen

You can't turn back the clock. But you can wind it up again.

Bonnie Prudden

The significant tense for human beings is the future tense.

Rollo May

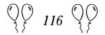

I don't like looking back. I'm looking ahead to the next show. It's how I keep young.

Jack Benny

There is one thing which gives radiance to everything. It is the idea of something around the corner.

G. K. Chesterton

To remain young, one must change.

Alexander Chase

Never run out of goals.

Earl Nightingale

Make it a rule of life never
to regret and never to look back.
Regret is an appalling waste of
energy; you can't build on it;
it's only good for wallowing in.
Katherine Mansfield

Success consists in the climb.
Elbert Hubbard

Ask the God who made you
to keep remaking you.
Norman Vincent Peale

For what has been —
thanks.
For what shall be —
yes.

Dag Hammarskjöld

Sources

Sources

Sources

Sources

Sources

About the Author

Criswell Freeman is a Doctor of Clinical Psychology living in Nashville, Tennessee. He is the author of *When Life Throws You a Curveball, Hit It* and *The Wisdom Series* from WALNUT GROVE PRESS. He is also the author of numerous quotation books published by DELANEY STREET PRESS.

About Delaney Street Press

DELANEY STREET PRESS is located in Nashville, TN. For more information about DELANEY STREET'S catalogue of inspirational titles, please call (800) 256-8584.